Hamlyn
20th Century
Style

Publishing Director: Laura Bamford
Executive Editor: Mike Evans
Assistant Editor: Humaira Husain
Production Controller: Melanie Frantz
Picture Research: Liz Fowler
Art Director: Keith Martin
Senior Designer: Geoff Borin
Design: Geoff Fennell

Consultant Editor: Emily Evans

First published in 1997 by Hamlyn,
an imprint of Reed Consumer Books Limited,
Michelin House, 81 Fulham Road,
London SW3 6RB
and Auckland, Melbourne, Singapore and Toronto

A Catalogue record for this book is available from the British Library
iSBN 0 600 59111 5

Printed and bound in China

leather
jackets

WAY OUT WEST

HON. W. F. CODY.

People have fashioned clothes from animal skins since the beginning of time, but the immediate predecessor to the modern leather jacket was the buckskin jacket worn by the pioneers of the old West. Like much so-called 'western' apparel, it was popularised in the early media by a handful of characters who wore it, most of whom were more fictional than factual although they were real people. William 'Buffalo Bill' Cody (previous page) who toured the world with his Wild West Show extravaganza had previously been (or so he was eager to remind the world) a trapper and at one-time an indian fighter. The celebrity which was largely self-created became the subject of dime novels, silent movies, talkies, comic books and a children's television series.

Considered to be the first 'adult' western film, Alan Ladd's portrayal of the lone-avenger *Shane* (above) consolidated the association of buckskin with the pioneering spirit of the West.

Like Cody, Davy Crockett was an actual historical figure, but his world-wide fame was posthumous. A hero at the siege of the Alamo of 1836, the 1950s saw – promoted by a Walt Disney film and kids' tv show – a children's craze for the racoon (complete with tail) Davy Crockett hat. Above, wearing the hat and the accompanying buckskin, John Wayne in his role as Crockett in the 1960 movie *The Alamo*.

FLYING ACES

WORLD WAR I

While foot soldiers were slaughtered by the million in the mud below, a romantic view of the First World War was to be found up in the skies where for the first time in history fighting men took to the air in their flying machines. The Allies' most celebrated – and decorated – flying ace was the Canadian Billy Bishop, but the name that epitomised these first leather-clad gladiators of the air was the German 'Red Baron' Manfred Von Richtofen (left), who scored 80 direct hits downing Allied planes. it established the airman as a true hero-figure of the 20th Century, to be confirmed twenty years later with the onset of World War ii.

SKY PILOTS

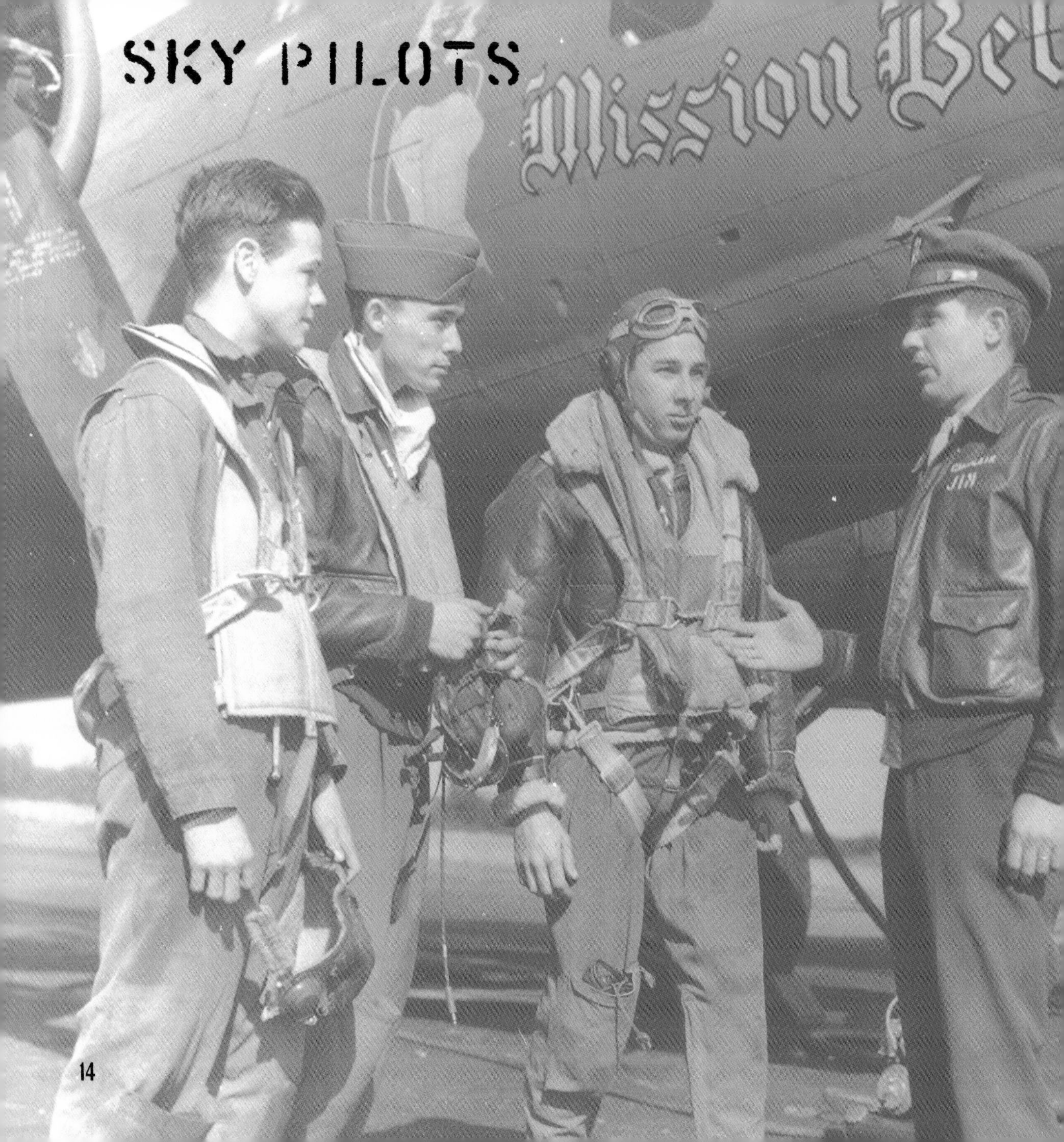

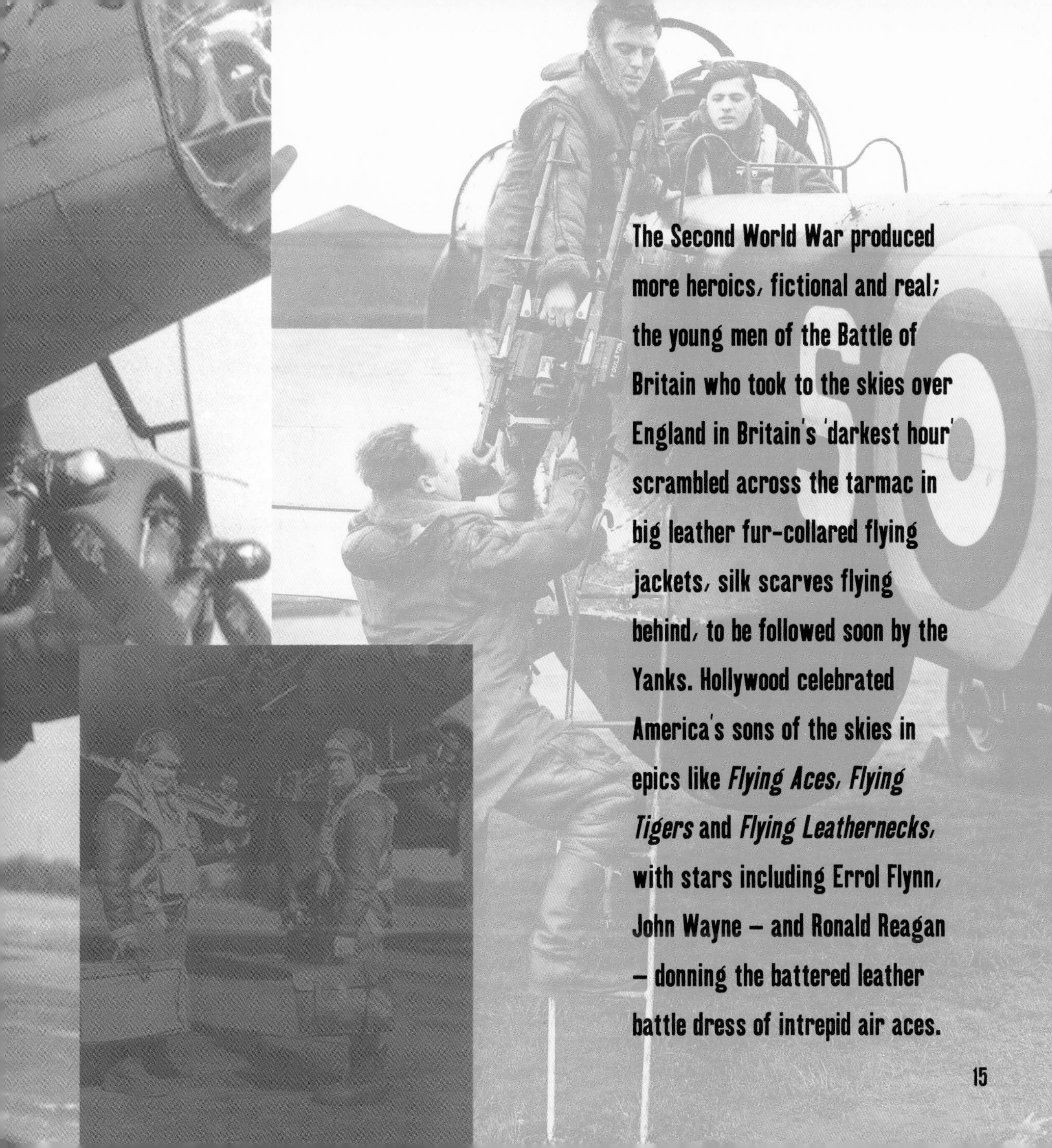

The Second World War produced more heroics, fictional and real; the young men of the Battle of Britain who took to the skies over England in Britain's 'darkest hour' scrambled across the tarmac in big leather fur-collared flying jackets, silk scarves flying behind, to be followed soon by the Yanks. Hollywood celebrated America's sons of the skies in epics like *Flying Aces, Flying Tigers* and *Flying Leathernecks*, with stars including Errol Flynn, John Wayne – and Ronald Reagan – donning the battered leather battle dress of intrepid air aces.

WOMEN AVIATORS

Between the wars, the aerial heroes were as often heroines. Female long-distance flyers like Amy Johnson (opposite, centre) who was the first woman to fly solo from England to Australia, and Amelia Earhart (left) who made the first female solo flight of the Atlantic and subsequently disappeared on a round-the-world attempt in 1937, also pioneered the girls-in-leather look while they were at it.

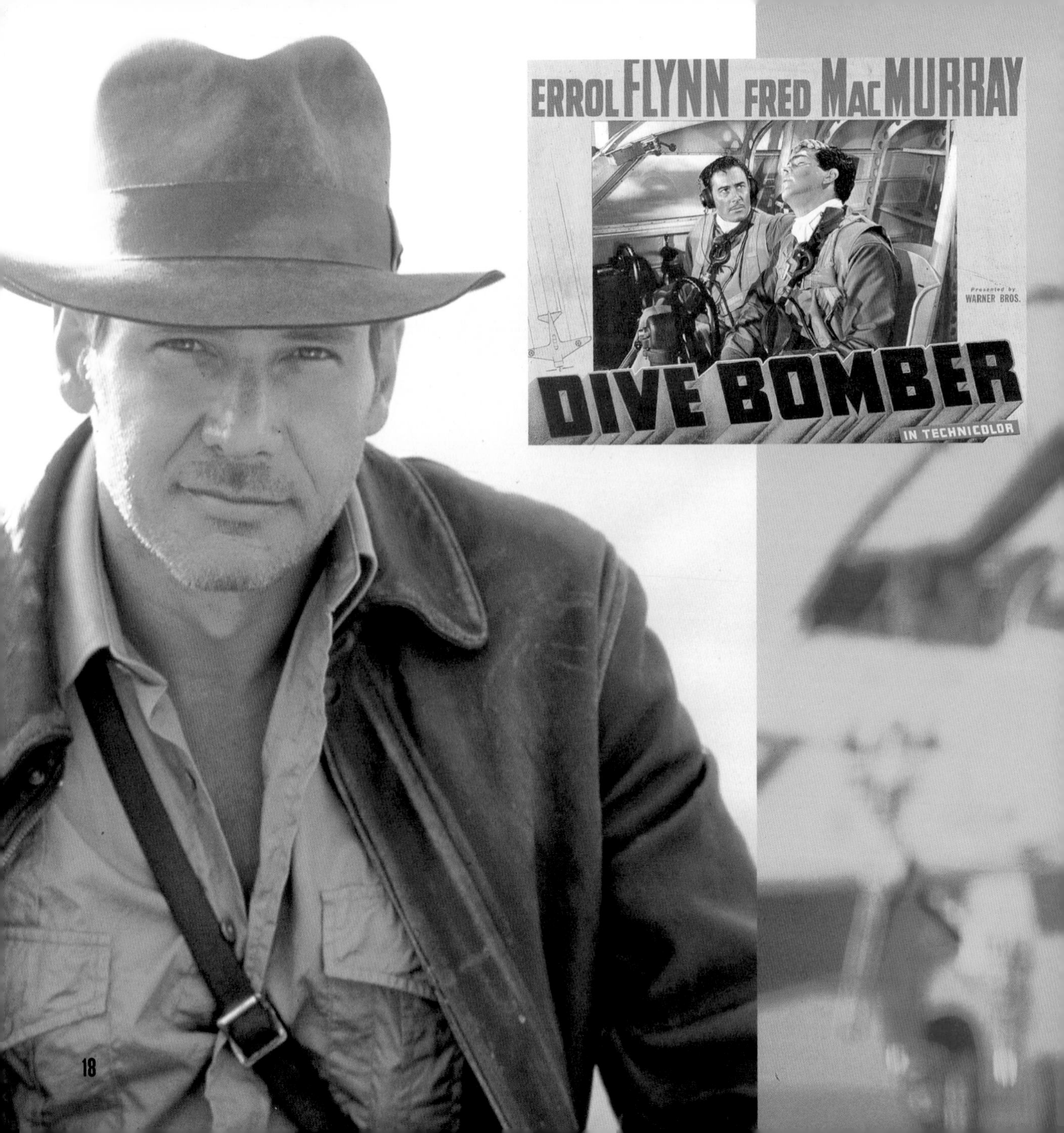
ERROL FLYNN FRED MacMURRAY
Presented by
WARNER BROS.
DIVE BOMBER
IN TECHNICOLOR

Contemporary movie-makers have continued to acknowledge the leather-jacket glamour of the air, including the Thirties-styled comic-strip adventures of Indiana Jones with Harrison Ford (opposite) and the ultra-glamour of the *Top Gun* stars Tom Cruise and Kelly McGillis.

NAZIS AND NASTIES

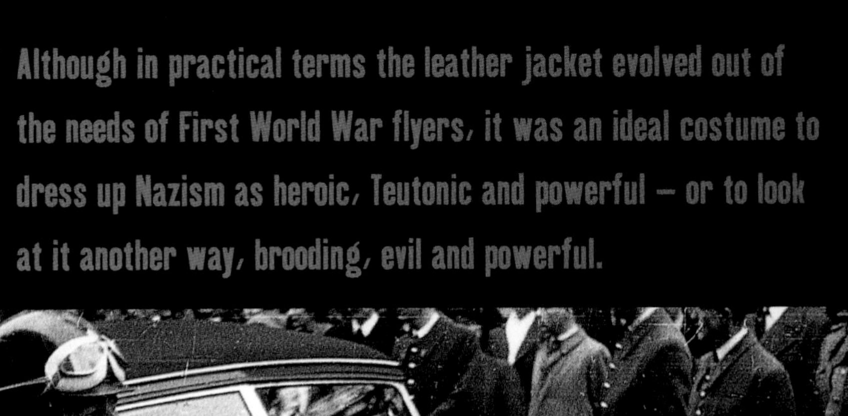

Although in practical terms the leather jacket evolved out of the needs of First World War flyers, it was an ideal costume to dress up Nazism as heroic, Teutonic and powerful – or to look at it another way, brooding, evil and powerful.

INTO THE FUTURE

Fictional tough guys also suggested that leather often meant meaner, from the stylish hoodlums of the Forties films to futuristic avengers like Mel Gibson's *Mad Max* (left) and of course Arnold Schwarzenegger's *Terminator*.

THE

LEADERS OF
THE PACK

From the ghostly nightriders transporting Jean Cocteau's *Orphee* into a 20th century Underworld, through Marlon and Marvin's rival gangs in *The Wild One* to real-life smalltown terrorisers epitomised by California's Hells Angels, leather-jacketed motorcyclists have always spelt trouble.

The smell of the greasers, the roar of the engines, as the bikers hit town.

Despite Marianne Faithfull's soft-erotic movie *Girl On A Motorcycle*, it's always been a man's man's world where Angels hound the Hippies and Rockers maul the Mods, though androgynous motorbike molls have invariably followed the Leader of the Pack in indentikit leathers.

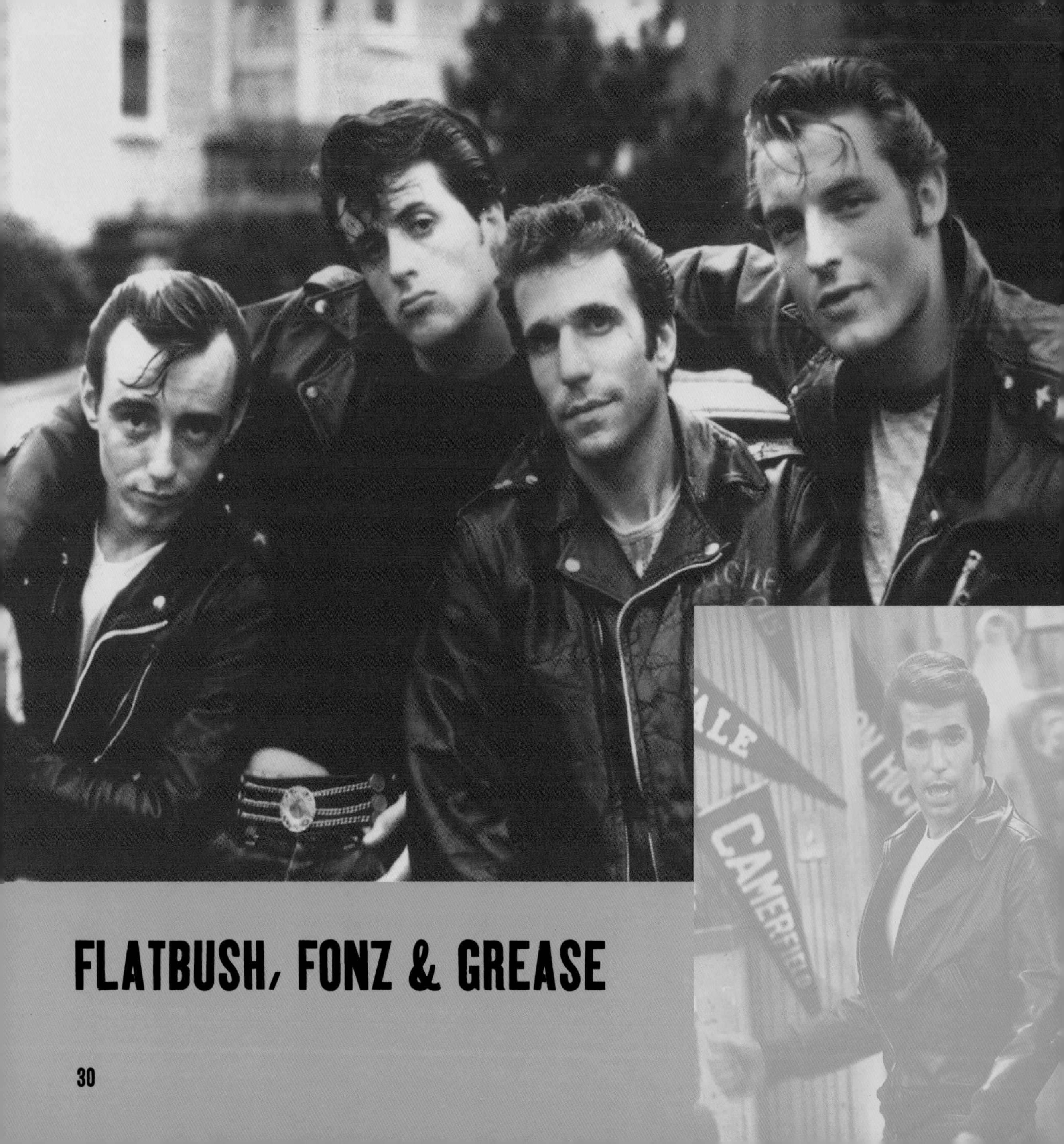

FLATBUSH, FONZ & GREASE

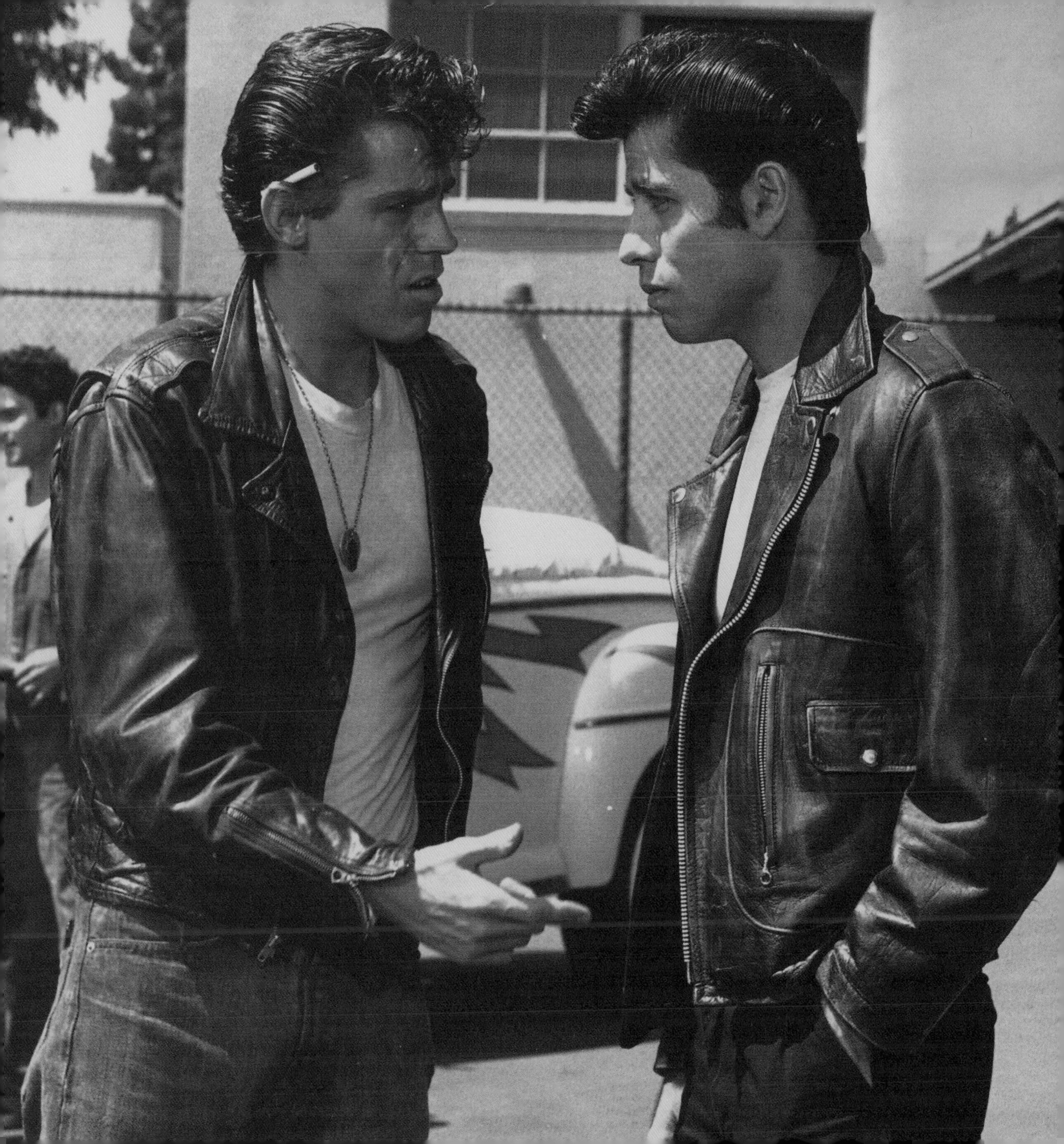

EASY RIDER

Teen exploitation pics featured a lotta leather over the years, from the sublime *Cool And Crazy* to the ridiculous *Hot Rod Rumble* in the 1950s, reaching its apogee in the 1966 motopsycho masterpiece by Hollywood's King 'B' Roger Corman *The Wild Angels* (opposite, right). '*Angels* featured Nancy Sinatra and Peter Fonda, who went on to make his own biker's odyssey in the first of the Seventies genre of road movies, the seminal *Easy Rider* (right).

ROCK ICONS

RENÉ CHATEAU presents

ELVIS PRESLEY

KING CREOLE

directed by
MICHAEL CURTIZ · produced by HAL WALLIS

with CAROLYN JONES · WALTER MATTHAU · DOLORES HART · DEAN JAGGER · VIC MORROW

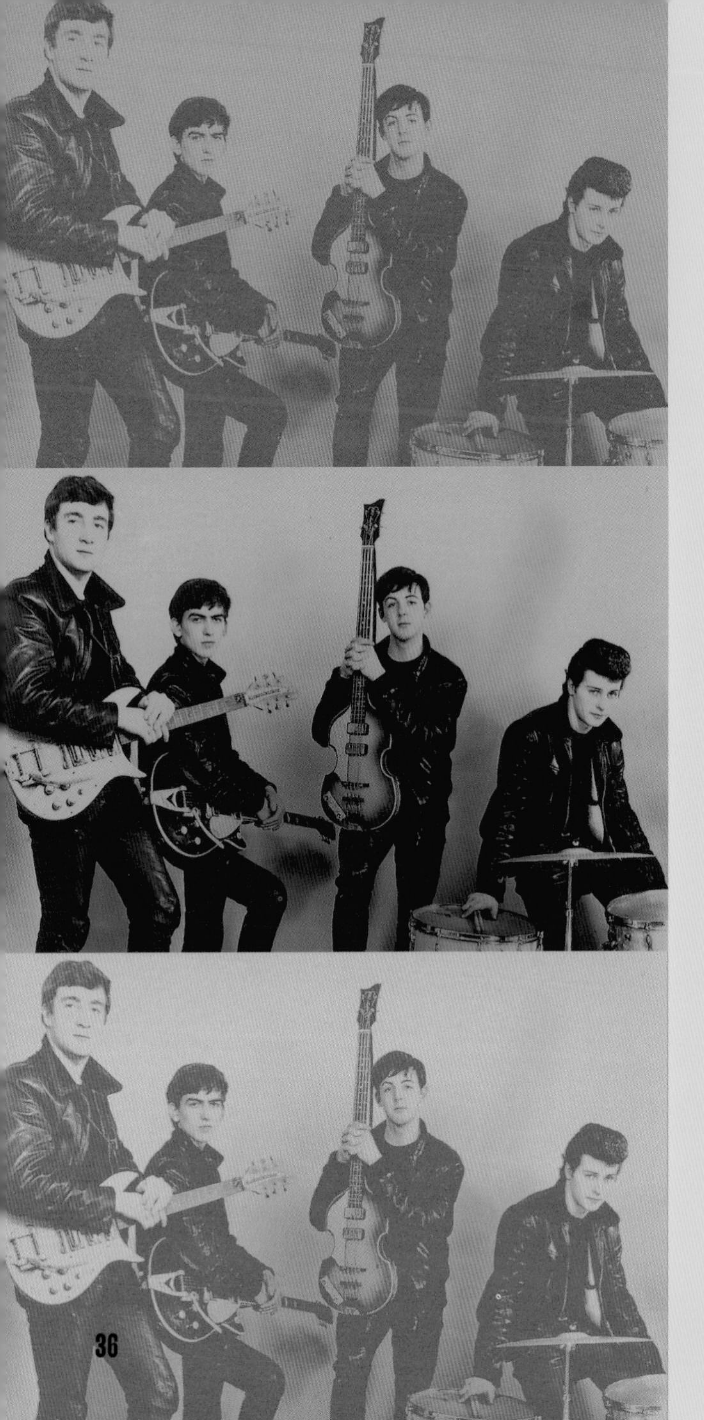

The earliest image of the Beatles, when they played the Hamburg cellar clubs, was partly created by local photographer Astrid Kirchherr, who encouraged the flat haircuts, moody pictures .....and black leather.

Although his initial hit-making hey-day saw Gene Vincent in neat slacks and flat sports cap (in fact his backing band were called the Blue Caps), his notoriety as a performer came with a series of UK-based 'comebacks' in the mid Sixties when, having injured his leg permanently in an auto accident, he struck a devilish pose in head-to-toe black leather.

After all those dire Hollywood movies throughout the 60's, it was significant that the most enduring image that Elvis adopted on his legendary 1968 'comeback' television special was of the leather jacketed rocker, a personality he'd turned his back on for the best part of a decade.

Wimp, wannabee or weirdo ? Whichever way you look at Jim Morrison, the all-leather look was a bit of a come-on; could anybody be taken seriously in those pants ?

Although the antithesis of rock'n'roll roughies and punk-rocker toughies, the more glam and glitzy – and sometimes camp – side of rock, which at various times included the likes of Freddy Mercury, David Bowie, Lou Reed (left) and George Michael (right), was always pretty heavy on the leather.

Fetish Fashion

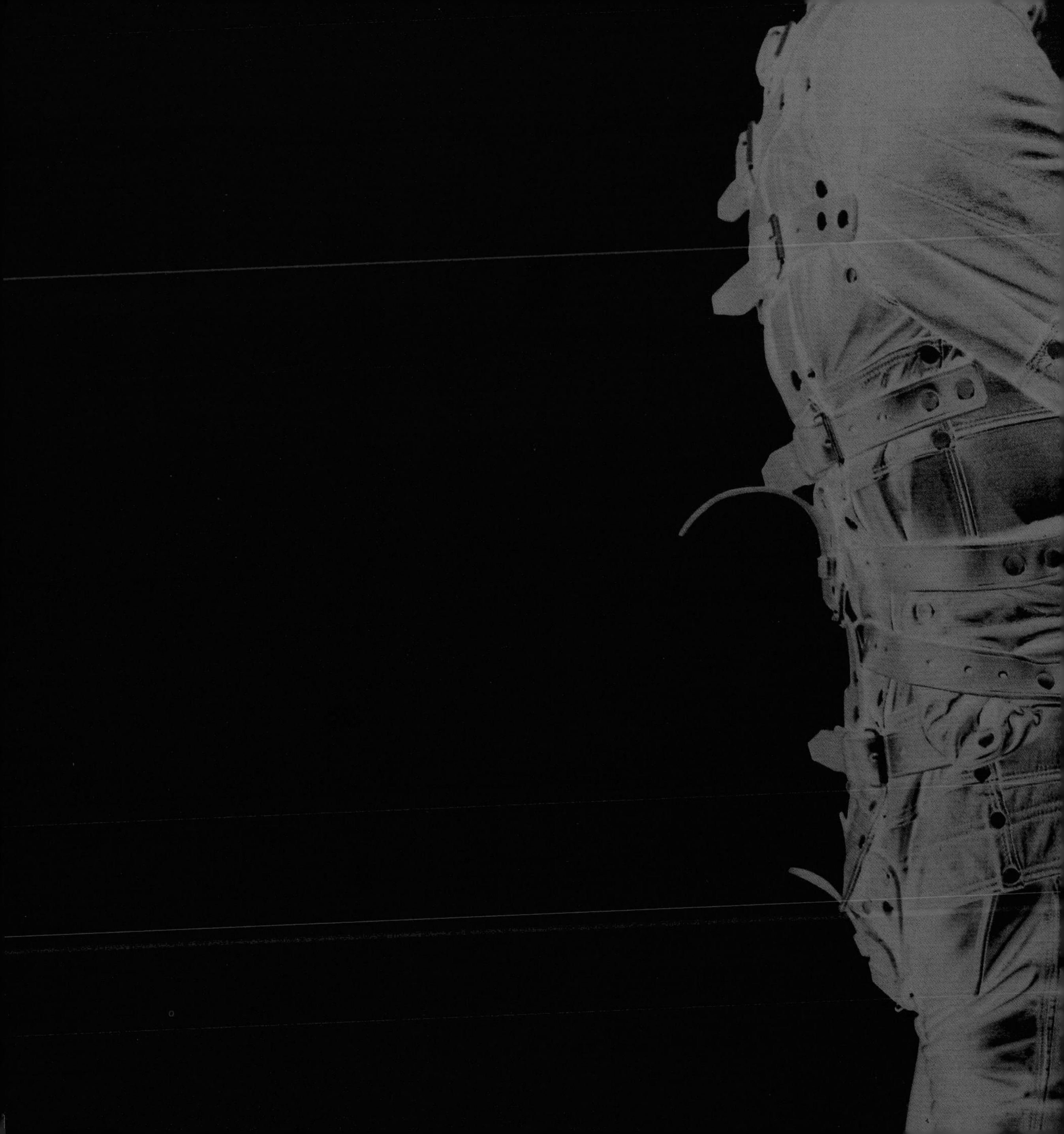

Leather jackets have been central to skin and bondage fetishism, straight and gay, from the Sixties softcore send-ups like *The Avengers* (left), the high camp *Modesty Blaise* and Marianne Faithfull's *Girl On A Motorcycle* (right), to the real thing in S&M society everywhere.

Whips 'n' Zips

Hey Punk!

PisTOLs
"ANARCHY IN
THE U.K"

Sid and Nancy

When punk first raised it's spiky head from the Kings Road enclave of Malcolm McLaren and Vivienne Westwood's shop Sex, along with the bondage gear, safety pins and torn T-shirts the common denominator dress-wise was the black leather jacket. Earlier than the Brit punk explosion, mid-seventies New York rockers including the Ramones, Blondie and their followers at Max's Kansas City and CBGB's made the BLJ their stamp of disapproval of the dinosaurs of the rock music establishment.

London Calling

And twenty years later, nouveau-punks parade around central London and the other big city centres still relying on black leather as a trade mark to go with the now generally discarded safety pins.

Leather

Couture

Regular clothes designers have long flirted with leather, from the practical outerwear shown in the 'Rodney' advert on the left – which was addressed to 'Mr. He-man'! – to the high fashion for smart ladies as evidenced in the *Vogue* advert for Harrods (far right) from 1927.

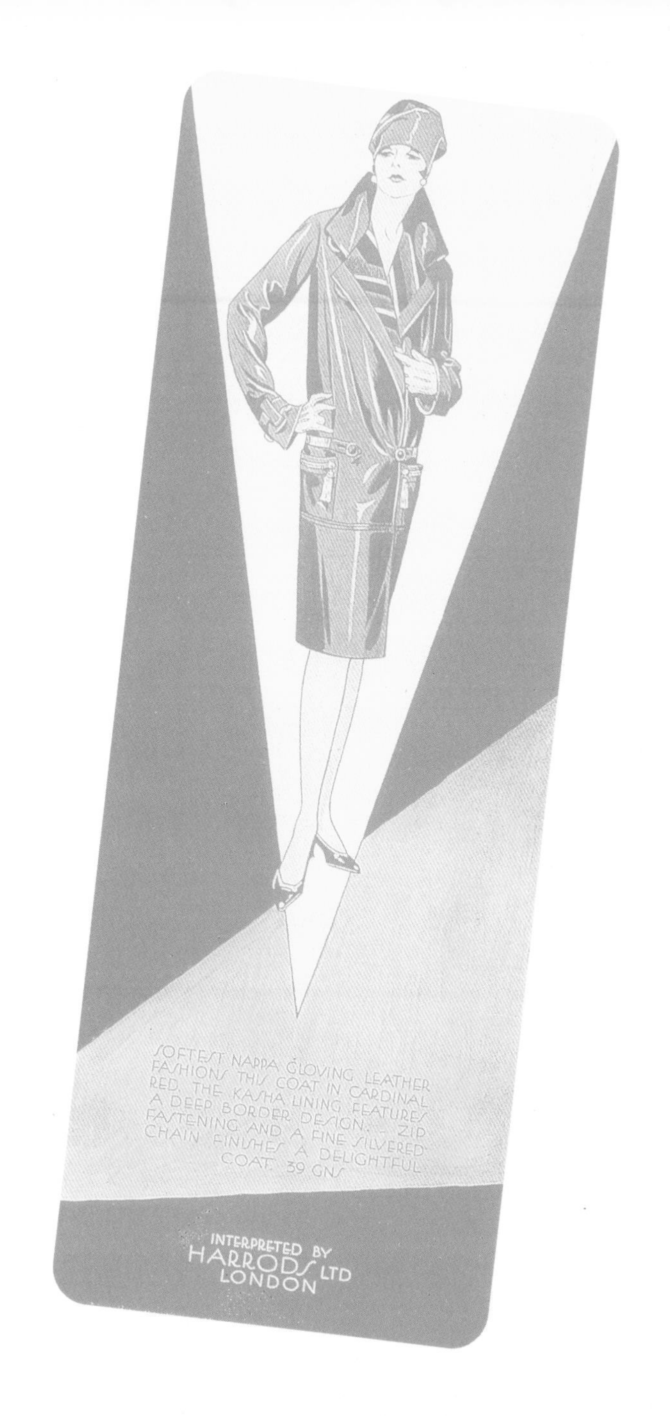
SOFTEST NAPPA GLOVING LEATHER
FASHIONS THIS COAT IN CARDINAL
RED. THE KASHA LINING FEATURES
A DEEP BORDER DESIGN. - ZIP
FASTENING AND A FINE SILVERED
CHAIN FINISHES A DELIGHTFUL
COAT. 39 GNS
INTERPRETED BY
HARRODS LTD
LONDON

The Swinging Sixties took leather in its stride fashion-wise, with numbers as extreme as the man's long jacket (left) worn with a typical floppy cap of the period and featured in Vogue in 1968, and the two-piece clearly influenced by *The Avengers* (right) which had appeared the year before.

in the post-punk Eighties the BLJ was prominent on the international catwalks as never before. An initial influence was Vivienne Westwood as she moved from the Kings Road cultism of the Sex shop to take punk onto the world's stage. When Westwood moved into other territories completely, the mainman leather-wise for a while was Jean-Paul Gaultier, and into the Nineties other designer labels that have made a mark with leather have included Versace, Sonia Rykiel, DKNY, Hermes (left) and Red or Dead (right).

Haut Couture leather in the Nineties:

Pages 54&55 – Paco Rabanne.

This page, clock-wise from top left – Red or Dead, Janet Howard, DKNY and Versace.

Opposite, clock-wise from top left – Versace, Sonia Rykiel, Chanel, DKNY, Dolce & Gabbana and Complice.

ACKNOWLEDGEMENTS

ADVERTISING ARCHIVES 56
AQUARIUS PICTURE LIBRARY 9, 11, 18 inset, 21, 25, 44, 64, /Paramount 18/19
ARCHIVE PHOTOS 9, 22,/Express Newspapers 28,/Kennedy 29
THE CONDE NAST PUBLICATIONS LTD/Harrods/British Vogue 57, /Patrick Hunt/British Vogue 59,/Peter Rand/British Vogue 58
CORBIS-BETTMANN 22/23
FETTERS 43
RONALD GRANT ARCHIVE 32 inset, 35, 46
HAMLYN 15 right,/Associated Press 17 inset,/Elvis Presley Enterprises 38,/Imperial War Museum 12 inset
HULTON GETTY PICTURE COLLECTION 16 inset,/Steve Eason 49, /Harry Todd 28
IMAGES COLOUR LIBRARY endpapers
KOBAL COLLECTION 30 inset,/A.I.P. 32,/Columbia 33,/Ebbets Field Film 30,/Mid-Atlantic/Ares/Claridge 45,/Paramount 8, /Para-Lucasfilm 18,/Paramount 31,/Twentieth Century Fox 22 inset,/Warner 24
CHRIS MOORE front cover flap, 61, /Chanel 63 top right, /Complice 62/63,/DKNY 62 bottom right, 63 bottom right, /Dolce & Gabbana 63 bottom centre left,/Hermes 60, /Red or Dead 62 top left,/S. Rykiel 63 top centre, /Versace 62 bottom left, 63 left
DON MORLEY 26
PETER NEWARK'S AMERICAN PICTURES 7, 12, 13, /Charles M. Bell 6,/Columbia Pictures 33 inset
REDFERNS/Glen A. Baker Archives 41,/Dave Ellis 40/41, /Gems 2/3,4/5,/K&K Studios 36,/Elliot Landy 39, /David Redfern 37,/Ebet Roberts 50, 53
RETNA/Rose Chancer 47,/Bill Davilla 62 top right, /Robert Fairer 54 /55, /Ray Stevenson 51, 52
SELFRIDGES ARCHIVES 16
SYGMA 14/15, 15 inset
VINTAGE MAGAZINE CO 17

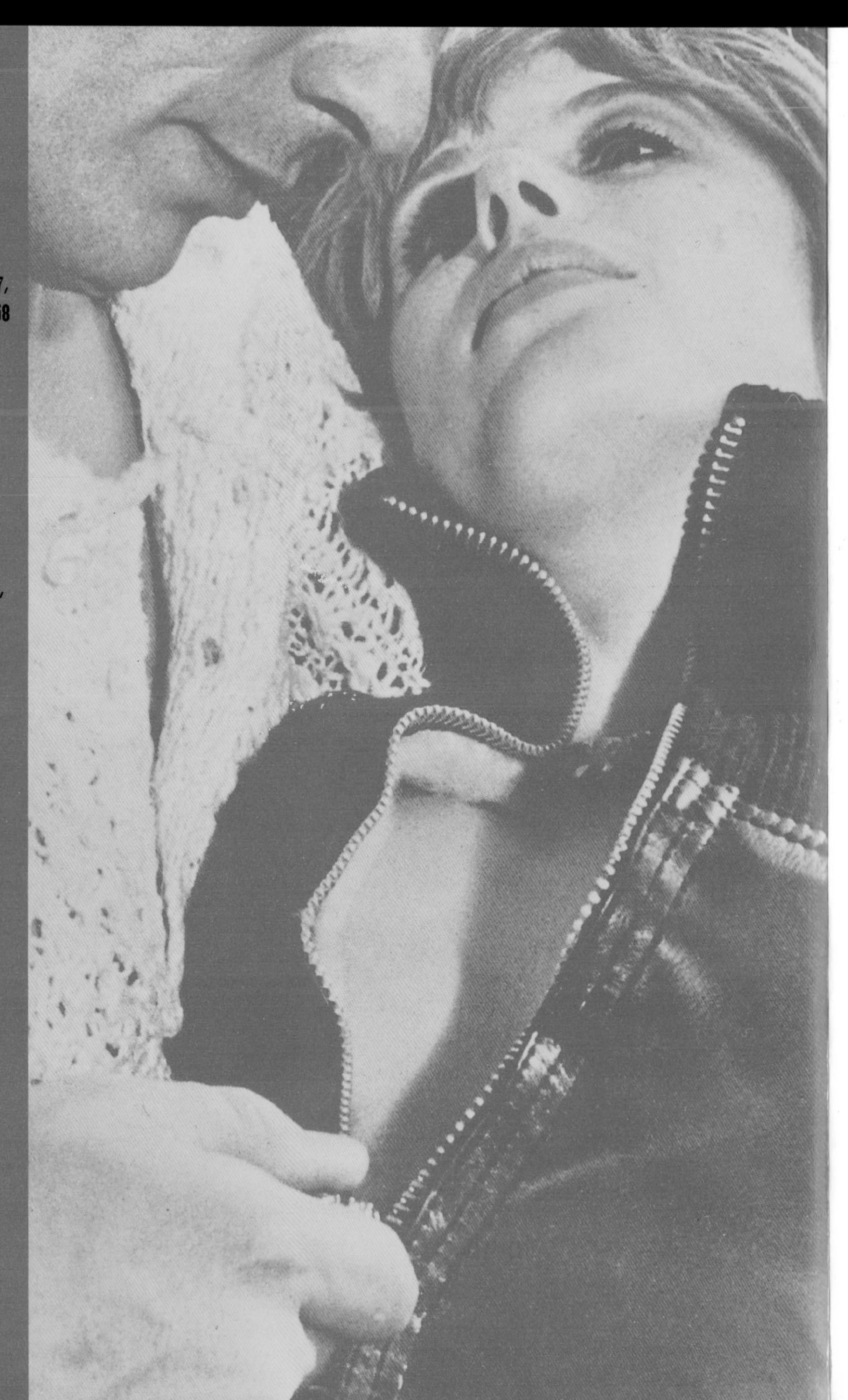

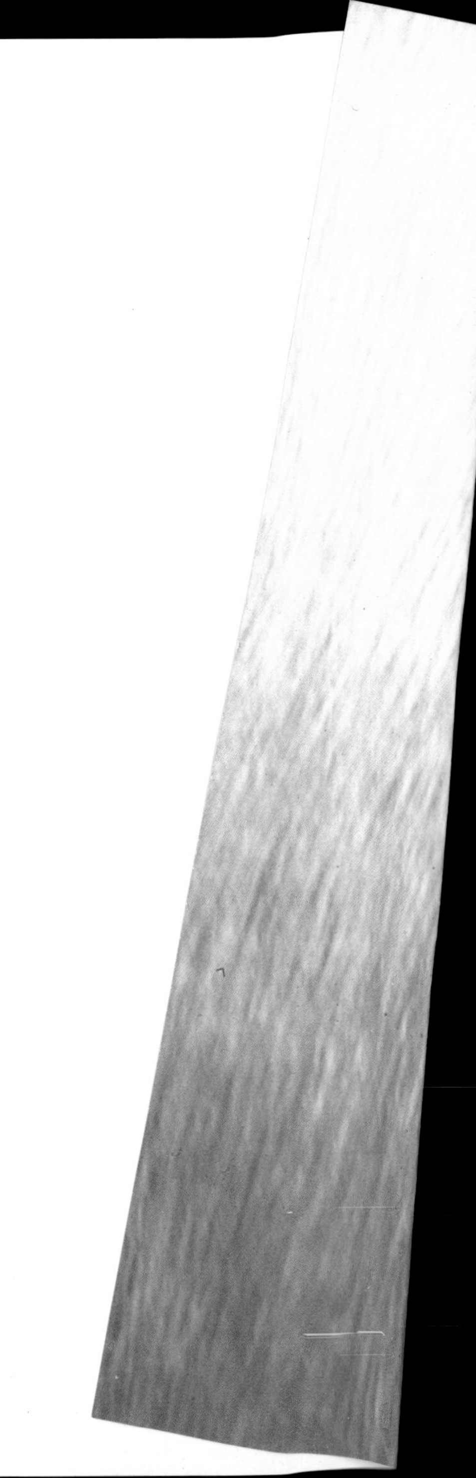